Playbook of Healthy Time Management

The Real Estate Playbook Series

Stacey Alcorn & Andrew F. Armata

AuthorHouse™
1663 Liberty Drive, Suite 200
Bloomington, IN 47403
www.authorhouse.com
Phone: 1-800-839-8640

© 2009 Stacey Alcorn & Andrew F. Armata. All rights reserved.

No part of this book may be reproduced, stored in a retrieval system, or transmitted by any means without the written permission of the author.

First published by AuthorHouse 5/5/2009

ISBN: 978-1-4389-4385-5 (sc)
ISBN: 978-1-4389-4386-2 (hc)

Printed in the United States of America
Bloomington, Indiana

This book is printed on acid-free paper.

To Justin, Abby, Adam
"Don't tell us the sky's the limit when there are footprints on the moon."

Contents

Foreword	ix
Important – Must Read	xi
Chapter One The Procrastination Principle	1
Chapter Two Time Mapping	5
Chapter Three Be The Early Bird	13
Chapter Four Mapping Time with Hit Lists and Quick Lists	17
Chapter 5 Delegate Your Plate	25
Chapter 6 Prioritizing… Easy as 1, 2, 3!	41
Chapter 7 Time Blocking – Be Your Own Client	47
Chapter 8 Multi-Tasking and Non-Event Planning	57
Chapter 9 The Pacman Problem	61
Chapter 10 Technology and Time	67
In Closing	71
Words to Live By…	73
About the Authors	89

FOREWORD

Everyone that is living on this earth gets the same 24 hours a day, the same 1440 minutes a day and the same 86,400 seconds a day. It does not matter if you are the President of the United States, a professional athlete or if you are an hourly laborer. Further, if you are in business for yourself as an owner or on a hundred percent commission income program, how you utilize your time can be the difference between success and failure, earning a million dollars or twenty thousand. It also could be the difference between how strong your relationships are and whether you feel fulfilled or constantly stressed out.

There have been thousands of books written on the subject of time management over the last twenty years but no matter whom the author is the success formula is very clear to me. A time management system should be simplistic and easy to execute. Further, it has to focus on three primary areas: your family life, your professional life and your own self-development. For twenty plus years I have owned a successful real estate firm, I have been part owner of a mortgage company, I have been part owner of an insurance company, I have sat on numerous boards, I have coached my three kids and participated in the important events in the life of a family. I am not Superman but I have been able to follow a daily routine that allows the most important events to be the most important things I do daily.

Stacey and Andy own countless successful companies and it seems like they add a new one every month. Once again, they have taken their real estate and mortgage company and developed a time management program that real estate sales associates and mortgage originators can relate to. The magic of the book however is that staff personnel and anyone in any industry can apply the strategies they have outlined. How many of us have procrastinated or developed a multitude of lists or have done something that could have been delegated. We all have. This book deals with all those issues plus it focuses on the strategies of how to time map, time block, and multi-task plus so much more.

Stacey and Andy you have done it again-keep the books coming because your sharing is making all of us in the industry better—Thanks.

Jeff Wright
RE/MAX Right Choice
Trumbull, CT

Important – Must Read

Ok, so if you are reading this book, you have taken a grand step toward mastering one of life's most difficult tasks- *time management*. Recognizing this area of your life needs some assistance is probably the most important key in improving in this area. We own and manage a multi-office real estate firm with hundreds of sales associates in addition to a thriving mortgage brokerage firm which is home to several top mortgage originators. We have met and worked with thousands of great real estate agents and mortgage originators throughout the country and there is one commonality we have noticed. Everyone of these individuals has struggled with time management. Those that have come the closest to mastering the art of time are most successful both in business and in life. What we mean by that is that we have seen many real estate agents and mortgage originators become multi-millionaires in their careers, not because they could manage time, but because they could not. Sales people such as this are unable to perfect their time management skills sufficiently enough in order to live a well balanced life.

Normally, those with time management problems earn less income, have less savings, have less time with their families, have relationship problems, and eventually all this leads to a blow to ones self esteem which means that the problems only snowball into bigger issues and eventually into crises status. For every twenty people we have met that have time management issues that lead to such life crises status, there is one that is the biggest producer, makes the most money, and appears to live the life many dream of. In countless instances, these people have even greater time management problems then the rest of us. We often see these types of sales people working eighty hours a week, running around at the whim of their clients, and sacrificing everything, including relationships, health and mental well being for their careers.

The average human will have approximately seventy years on this earth. That amounts to less than four thousand weeks in total. When you sit and contemplate that, it is not a lot of time. In fact, some will not be allotted that much time and others will be granted much more. Since you will never know for sure how much time you have, it is important not to squander any. This book is designed to help real estate agents and mortgage originators time mange their careers, relationships, and personal well being into a life worth living. The fact is that you CAN have everything you ever wanted in life as long as you properly manage the one thing that makes every human equal, *time*.

So, before we start, we ask you to do us one favor. Since you have already made it through three entire paragraphs in this book, you clearly recognize that time management is an area of your life you need to improve upon. One thing that we have learned as individuals who have struggled with time management issues our entire lives, is that when we run out of time we usually cut out of our lives some of the most important things. Right now, this book is your lifesaver. You can not afford to not finish the book. Therefore, we ask you to take out your calendar right now. Set aside one hour a day for the next week to read this book. You will learn some effective ways of setting aside time by reading this book to the end. However, on the very first day that you do not stick to your daily reading schedule… AND THIS IS IMPORTANT…. On that day, take this book and put it on the back of your toilet seat. I know you are thinking we are completely nuts right now. However, we understand how easy it is to lose time and for many of you, if you miss a day or two in reading this book, it is over. You will not pick it up again and you will not think twice about it until ten years down the road when you are struggling in life because you have no savings, no spouse, no relationships, poor health, and more time to yourself then you really want. We do not want that to happen to you. Do us a favor and do yourself a favor, read the book consistently every single day. The first day that you do not read it, stick the book on the back of your toilet seat because if you only get five free minutes a day while you are on the toilet, well, gosh darn it… use that time effectively and get through this book.

> **Tip:** If you lose your reading momentum then immediately put this book on the back of your toilet seat so that you will eventually find the time to get through it.

Chapter One
The Procrastination Principle

So, where do we begin to tackle the lack of time that we all face each day? A good place to start is with your mental attitude about time and how to handle it. Have you ever had one of those days where your alarm clock went off and as you got up and made your coffee and visited the lavatory you thought about all the things you had to do that day. Two different clients want you to show them properties at the same time. Then there is that call you had to make to another client telling them their offer was rejected. You also have a home inspection, a mortgage commitment due, smoke detectors to install, and a final water reading. Then you remember your son's dentist appointment at three o'clock. You have got that parent teacher conference at five o'clock. Also, was today the day you had enrolled in a continuing education class with the local board? *Did you ever have one of these mornings?* It is one of these mornings where you are completely overwhelmed before you even turn on the shower. Unfortunately, we have had more than our share of these types of mornings. Every once and a while we choose to take a morning like this and just throw in the towel and take the entire day off from work!

That, by the way, is not always a bad idea but with the aid of this book you should be able to keep days like this at a minimum.

The fact is that many of us get so overwhelmed just by the thoughts of everything we must accomplish in a day that we lose even more time just by thinking about it. Whether you realize it or not, you lose time in these situations for two reasons; physical procrastination and mental procrastination, or as we like to call it, The Procrastination Principle. That's right, you actually deduct time from your day by both your physical and mental reaction to being overwhelmed by the lack of time available to you. You lose time because your body is physically wired to procrastinate, whereby your body will move and react at a slower rate of speed based on the anxiety you feel about the day. When you are overwhelmed and feel nervous, your shower will take a little longer, you will walk a little slower, and you will move at a lingering pace when getting ready. Sometimes when we tell people this they find it difficult to believe. You think, "Well, I have so much to do, I am going to get ready for work as fast as possible." In reality, we can not lie to our bodies. If we are overwhelmed and feel like there is a lack of time our bodies physically cannot be tricked into moving faster.

Try this exercise if you are skeptical: For the next week time how long it takes you to get out of the house each day. On a piece of paper, write the time when your alarm clock goes off and then write the time as you leave the house. Being in the real estate or mortgage business we can almost guarantee you will have one of THOSE mornings where you wake up feeling overwhelmed by the amount of things you must get done in a day. Even if you are mentally unaware of it, your body will physically move slower and you will take longer to get ready to leave the house on that day. Now multiply that time you lost by five, six, or even ten times when you bring the overwhelmed feeling to the office with you.

In addition to the physical procrastination that our bodies will experience, a good majority of us will also suffer from mental procrastination. Most of you know exactly what we are talking about. You know your day is going to be miserable because you have too much to do so you watch the news before you leave the house, you stop for a coffee, read the newspaper, and you sit in the parking lot of the office to hear what song's next on the radio. When you finally do get to work you take time to talk to your co-workers as you shuffle to your desk, you send an email to a friend to see what is going on for the weekend, you even might play a quick game of solitaire on your computer. In fact, you will do just about anything before having to face the massive amount of personal and work related chores you must get done by the end of the day. The Procrastination Principle leads you astray and before you know it you have squandered away a very valuable chunk of your time.

Later in this book, we will talk about time mapping, listing, delegating, prioritizing, time blocking, and multi-tasking where you will learn ways to use your first hour of the day to organize your workload mentally while tending to your morning rituals. However, before we even get there we are going to give you an extremely valuable piece of knowledge. If you use this tidbit wisely, you will easily collect for yourself upwards of seven hours, and maybe even more, in a given week. Are you ready for this? THIS IS IMPORTANT TO UNDERSTAND. It is important because if we can help you save even one hour per day, then that is seven hours in a week and 364 hours in a year which amounts to more than nine entire days of extra time throughout the year. Could you use a week's vacation? Then listen up!

Here goes…. Whether you know it or whether you do not know it, you have MORE THEN ENOUGH TIME TO GET EVERYTHING DONE EACH AND EVERY DAY. That's right! You have more then enough time. You must constantly remind yourself of this and use this revelation to calm your nerves when you feel overwhelmed by time constraints. As soon as you have one of those mornings where you are feeling nervous, edgy, and overwhelmed, all you have to do is look in the mirror and say, "I have more then enough time today to get everything done and I think I will even have some ME time." Say it ten times in the mirror while you are getting ready.

If you start each morning with this kind of mental attitude, you will not squander time because you will look at time as a manageable asset to your business and your life. We both remind ourselves four or five times throughout the day that we have more then enough time to get everything done and that we will probably end up with some free time by days end. If you focus on this statement throughout your day you will be able to take on any challenge calmly and swiftly. You will look forward to getting your chore list done so that you can steal a little YOU time at the end of the day. What is even better is you will feel good throughout the day and much of your stress will disappear. Most of the stress we feel is because we doubt our ability to conquer our given chore list throughout the day. If you already know in your head that you have more then enough time to complete every task you have committed to, then what is there to stress about?

> **Tip:** You will save yourself hours of time each week if you start each day with a great mental attitude. You DO have more then enough time to complete everything you committed to do each and every day!

Chapter Two
Time Mapping

If you were going to drive across the country you probably would not leave the house without a map or some sort of navigation system. Why do you need the map if you know that driving North will get you where you want to go? Because driving North may not actually get you where you want to end up and, if by chance it does, you are not going to get there in the most efficient manner possible. The map is our guide to our final destination. Our daily time schedule is the map of our days, weeks, and years. You should never start your day without a map of where you are going to spend your precious time.

In order to properly manage your time you have to figure out what you want to do with your life. This involves coming up with a very basic pie chart of what areas of your life you would ideally spend most of your time. How much time do you want to spend at work each week? We have met so many real estate agents and loan originators who tell us that they can not control the number of hours they work because some weeks are busy and some weeks are slow and if a buyer, seller, or borrower needs them then they must respond. What you will learn in this book is that everyone, including real estate agents and mortgage originators, has much more control over his or her time then they think and it is possible to map out time for every important aspect of life each and every week.

Once you have figured out how much time you need for work, then figure out how much time you need to fulfill your spiritual needs. This might include meditation or visiting a church or synagogue. How much family time do you need? If you could have the perfect schedule each week, how much time would you want to spend with your loved ones? This includes having dinner, going to the park, shopping, coaching baseball or soccer teams, visiting relatives, or even just spending time at home.

Aside from family time, it is important to partition some time each week to work on your relationship with a significant other or spouse. There is an epidemic in the real estate industry which has lead to extremely high divorce rates among real estate agents and loan originators. Take it from two people that have been surrounded by real estate professionals our entire careers. This profession leads to physical, emotional, and financial strains on many relationships. Every real estate agent and mortgage originator feels time constraints as they balance demanding careers, families, relationships, and finances. When there is not enough time in the day to do everything then more often then not there are two areas that we always delete from our daily calendar, personal time and relationship time. The other areas of our lives suffer for sure, but these two areas are usually obliterated from our time map all together. The result is failed relationships and low self esteem. The good news is that this will never happen to you because you are taking action by reading the Playbook of Healthy Time Management.

Please make sure that there is time mapped out each week for one-on-one time with your partner or spouse. Whether it is dinner alone, a movie, or a Sunday morning walk, this time alone with that special person is key to healthy time management. We have had many sales professionals tell us that time alone with their partner is near to impossible. They have families and they can not afford to get a baby sitter once a week to take care of the kids. The fact is, there is always some free time for you and your partner each week where you can spend time alone. If you can not do it later in the day, make a commitment to meet for lunch once a week. One of the benefits of a sales business is that we do have control over our schedules, so pencil your partner in every Monday for lunch! If you can not do that, then have a rented movie date once a week after the kids go to bed. Commit to it and stick to it! Remember at the beginning of the book we talked about the crises status that we will all face if we do not take control of our time? By rationing out time to build a relationship with your partner, you will have the support system you need to maintain a healthy balance to your life, which will make it much simpler to maintain the reigns over your time.

Next, you should allocate plenty of time each week to take care of the home front. This includes cleaning, grocery shopping, doctor and dentist appointments, running errands, appointments for your kids, preparing meals, and anything else you do on a weekly basis just to maintain your household.

ME time is the most important time of the week. It is imperative that you set aside some portion of your week just for you. Most of us put our own self interest at the bottom of everything we do. When we feel good about ourselves we excel in the other areas of our lives. This time might include going to the gym, reading, knitting, taking classes (fun classes like cooking, knitting, wood working), joining a book club, walking, watching television, drawing, or even just laying in bed. Whatever you enjoy doing make sure you do some of that every single week. Many who are reading this book can not even fathom taking time for themselves. Take baby steps if you must. Ration out some portion of your schedule for just you. Practice for a while. You will soon realize that those ME times that you have set aside will motivate you to accomplish more in your week. You will rush through some of the more mundane tasks in your life while looking forward to doing the things you enjoy, which means you will actually save time.

Last, it is important to have a time reserve each week. As sales professionals many of you will feel that the time reserve needs to be a large percentage of your time each week since we live at the whim of our clients. However, the reserve time can be as low as 5% of your week. With the skills you are learning in this book, you will find that you are NOT at the whim of your clients, and even at those times you choose to accommodate a client outside of your schedule, then you will be making up that time lost in one area of your life, NOT by dipping into your time reserve, but by taking that time back from the work area of your life. More often then not, the time reserve will pour over into one of the areas of your life you really enjoy, like family time, relationship time or me time.

Yours may look very different, but this is how a typical week might look for some:

50%	Work
5%	Spiritual
10%	Family Time
10%	Relationship Time
5%	Household
10%	Me Time
<u>10%</u>	Reserve Time
100%	Total

Next to the areas below write down the percentage of time you would like to dedicate each week to the following areas:

_____%	Work
_____%	Spiritual
_____%	Family Time
_____%	Relationship Time
_____%	Household
_____%	Me Time
_____%	Reserve Time
100%	Total

Now that you have recognized the areas where you would like to spend your time, you have to quantify that into hours and minutes. In order to do that, you will need to calculate how many free hours are in the day. This varies for everyone. How many waking hours do you have in a day? For us, we generally wake up at about 5:00 am every morning and we are usually in bed by 10:00 pm. That means we have 17 hours to work with each day. So when mapping out our week based on the previous time allotments, it would look something like this:

17 hours x 7 days = 119 hours

50% Work = 59.5 hours
5% Spiritual = 5.95 hours
10% Family = 11.9 hours
10% Relationship = 11.9 hours
5% Household = 5.95 hours
10% Me Time = 11.9 hours
10% Reserve = 11.9 hours
100% = Total

This time map may look completely different then yours. Someone who is single with no children will obviously have a very different time map then someone with a family. As well, some might choose to spend a much lower percentage of their day at work. There is no correct way at mapping a day, what is important is that you map it so that you base your time map on what you want to do with your life.

Once you have established how you want to divide up your time each week make yourself a weekly calendar and chart out areas where you are going to spend your time. This is the rough draft of your time schedule. When we get later on into the book we will take this exercise and expand upon it with something called time blocking. For now, we are just looking at the week and penciling in the areas where we are going to spend our time. Draw out a calendar or prepare one on your computer where you have one block of time for each hour of the day. Then figure out how many blocks you need for each of the areas of your life. For example, on our schedule we need approximately 60 hours set aside for work time. That equals 60 blocks. Once you have figured out how many blocks you need then block out an entire week. Block out all of your time except for your time reserve. The time reserve will eventually be filled in by one of the other areas of your life.

The Real Estate Playbook Series

WEEKLY SCHEDULE

	SUN	MON	TUES	WED	THURS	FRI	SAT
5:00 AM		Spiritual	Spiritual	Spiritual	Spiritual	Spiritual	Spiritual
6:00 AM	Household						
7:00 AM	Household	Work	Work	Work	Work	Work	Work
8:00 AM	Household	Work	Work	Work	Work	Work	Work
9:00 AM	Household	Work	Work	Work	Work	Work	Work
10:00 AM	Household	Work	Work	Work	Work	Work	Work
11:00 AM	Household	Work	Work	Work	Work	Work	Family
12:00 PM	Relationship	Me	Me	Me	Me	Me	Family
1:00 PM	Relationship	Work	Work	Work	Work	Work	Family
2:00 PM	Relationship	Work	Work	Work	Work	Work	Family
3:00 PM	Relationship	Work	Work	Work	Work	Work	Family
4:00 PM	Relationship	Work	Work	Work	Work	Work	Family
5:00 PM	Relationship	Work	Work	Work	Work	Work	Family
6:00 PM	Relationship	Work	Work	Work	Work	Work	Family
7:00 PM	Relationship	Relationship	Relationship	Relationship	Relationship	Me	Me
8:00 PM		Me	Me	Me	Me		Me
9:00 PM							

Upon completing this task, take time over the next week to see how accurate your schedule was. Each day take a few minutes to circle the hours where you did spend the time in the category you mapped out. After one week of studying your schedule, take notes on what you learned. You will have a clearer picture of the areas in your life where you are spending too much time. For example, maybe you planned on a 50 hour work week and you ended up at 63 hours. If that is the case, you need to study your schedule to figure out what areas of your life you dipped into to steal that 13 hours. Did you have 13 hours in your reserve pool? If not, then another area of your life suffered that week. Do this same exercise the following week but this time, adjust the blocks of time based on what you learned the week before. Start looking for areas where you have free time.

Each week post a copy of your hourly schedule on your refrigerator, your computer, your mirror, or anywhere else you spend large amounts of time. This will serve as a conscious reminder of the fact that your goal is to balance your time each week. There are always going to be areas of your life where it is easy to let your time get consumed. For us, we could stay hours and hours at work. However, when we have our time map sitting next to us at the office, it is our little reminder that there are other areas of our lives that are just as, or more important, as work. Sometimes that is all we need to pack it up and call it a day.

> **Tip:** Start mapping your time by the week to learn how balanced your life is. Map out time for every area of your life and stick to it.

Chapter Three
Be The Early Bird

In addition to running multiple real estate firms and a mortgage company, we spend some of each day managing a debt negotiating firm and our title company. That is four flourishing businesses we attend to regularly while at the same time managing our home lives and our health. Andy is a single dad and makes sure that he has plenty of one on one time with his son every week and manages to take every weekend to be with his son. Stacey decided to pursue a law degree in the evenings.

Much of the time management skills we practice today were developed from cramming in all the important business details for all of our businesses while maintaining a balancing act with our home, family, and schooling responsibilities. It has not been easy, and it probably never will be. However, there are skills we learned to cope with the time management dilemmas we regularly ran into.

In the past few years we have experienced a down turn in the real estate market in the Northeast. That has meant that we needed to spend as much time as possible cultivating mortgage business and keeping our real estate agents at our firms motivated, educated, and busy. As well, we recognized that in order to keep the real estate business profitable, we would have to spend much more time recruiting new agents into the firm. Needless to say, we could not dip into our work time even though Andy had a son to raise and Stacey was pursuing another degree. In short, we were forced to really analyze our weekly schedules to figure out where we were going to find the time to get everything done each day.

Have you ever heard the expression, "burning the midnight oil." That is a reference to people who are up and about all hours of the night. That used to be us working until all hours of the night to get everything done. The problem was that we would get home from work well after midnight on many evenings and then drag ourselves back to the office at nine or ten o'clock the next day. Early on we decided that this was no way to work. We always seemed to feel sluggish and tired and even though we were working late, we were not working efficiently. We then tried something different. Instead of going to bed at eleven o'clock or midnight, we each started going to bed at 10:00 and then waking up at 4am. After one week of this, we knew we would be able to run a much more efficient business and still have time to enjoy our lives after work. Andy was able to start making it home for dinner with his son. Stacey was able to study and read homework assignments and compete with students who did not have jobs.

When we started waking up at 4 am after six hours of solid sleep, both of us felt great. If we learned anything from our beginning years of running multiple businesses it was the importance of waking up early. We now both wake up every morning at 4:30 and we use those extra hours in our day to do things that we enjoy doing. That is our ME Time. Before we even get to work each day we spend and hour and a half reading, watching the news, or exercising. At one time in our lives we would have told you it was impossible for us to wake up that early every morning, only because we were so used to coming home and getting to bed after midnight. Now, we both look forward to our early mornings alone where we get to choose how to spend the quiet time.

There are two significant reasons why people are so productive at the wee hours of the morning. First, our bodies and minds are rejuvenated. If you enjoy reading, you will notice you read faster in the morning. Our eyes grow weary by late evening and it is difficult to retain information that we read. In the mornings, our eyes are re-vitalized so we can read quicker and the information we read creates a much longer impression in our minds. The other reason early risers have more productive time in their days is that for most of us, that early morning head start is the only time of the day where we are truly alone where we can accomplish tasks uninterrupted.

Think about how much time you have each day right now where you are 100% alone. No spouse, no children, no co-workers, no phone, no email, no anything. For most of us there is no time in the day where we are alone. We wake up when our spouse or kids wake up and then we are in constant communication with people the entire day until our head hits the pillow. That is one of the biggest challenges when it comes to time management, that our time is not really just ours. We share our time with hundreds of people every day. Imagine though, how much you could change your life if you had twelve hours a week that were just yours. Even if you had five hours a week to yourself, what could you do with it? It is time to find out!

Set your alarm clock to go off at 4:30 tomorrow morning. However, before you do that, decide now what you are going to do with the extra time. Are you normally up at 6:30? If so, you just added fourteen hours of your own time to your schedule. We strongly encourage you to make this time yours. Purchase that book you have been dying to read. Try writing your own book. Go to the gym. Take up a new hobby. Learn about the stock market. There are a million ways to fill the vacant time slots. Whatever you do, make it enjoyable. Within a few days you will have no problem waking up that early because you will really enjoy that time to yourself.

By the way, even though we have encountered a rough real estate market these past few years, we have had the time, energy, and ambition to add several new offices, as well as a mortgage brokerage firm, the title company, and a debt negotiating firm. The secret of our success during these past few years was waking up early, managing our time, and making plenty of time for the good stuff in life.

> **Tip:** Start being the early bird! Try setting your alarm clock for a 4:30 wake up call. Take those early mornings of alone time to read books, write, exercise, or anything else you enjoy.

Chapter Four
Mapping Time with Hit Lists and Quick Lists

Anyone with time management challenges will agree that one of the biggest trials each day is that no matter what we have planned out for ourselves, it is practically impossible to stick to the plan when someone else has intentions of taking some of our time. For example, Andy might decide that this morning he is going to work on returning calls from nine o'clock until noon. Well, what happens if he gets to the office and learns that the internet connection in the office is not working so nobody in the office is able to work? Even if he delegates this problem to someone else, the internet connection predicament is inevitably going to eat up a piece of his time. The good news is there are many things we can do to limit the amount of time that others dominate each day, but before we even get to that point, it is important that we map out all of our important daily and weekly goals so that when we are knocked off track each day, we will recognize it and then get right back on.

The easiest way to ensure that you will always get back into your daily schedule in an efficient manner is to make lists. There are several different ways to compose your lists each day to maximize efficiencies. The method that we both utilize and recommend involves a two step process which we call Hit Lists and Quick Lists. Here is how you do it. On Sunday evening, write down two or three major tasks that would make you feel fulfilled if you were to complete those tasks within the upcoming week. These responsibilities could be anything that you would feel really good about completing that week. It does not matter if the task is personal or business. All that matters is that you will feel good when it is done. For example, maybe the shrubs in front of your home have been overgrown for weeks. You look at them every day when you leave the house and when you come home. You asked your spouse to take care of the shrubs, but that was over a month ago. The shrubs just annoy you. Wouldn't you feel good to get the shrubs pruned? If so, then that is going to be on your Hit List for the week.

We find it important to have more than one major task on our Hit Lists each week. A good number is three. You do not want to have so many items on your weekly Hit List that they would eat up your entire week's time if you were to accomplish these items, you just need two or three items on there that will give you a good feeling once they have been completed. A second item on your Hit List for the week might be to book a vacation. Maybe you have been meaning to get that done for months and just never got to it. Put that on your Hit List then. So, before you go to bed Sunday evening, you have got two or three tasks you would like to complete for the week and you have written them down on your Hit List. As you go to sleep Sunday, picture yourself completing those tasks by Friday.

When Monday morning rolls around it is time to spend 5 minutes making your daily Quick List. This is everything you are going to accomplish by days end. The two of us do not write our lists until we get to the office. As we are getting ready throughout the morning, we start making mental notes of items we will include on the list. As soon as we sit at our desks at the office, we grab sticky notes and write our lists. I spend no more then 30 seconds each making our lists of what we will get done within our days.

Many books on time management that will tell you to keep an ongoing list in your day planner and whenever you think of something you need to do you just add it to your list. This may work for you. It may not work for some because in order to be an efficient business person we need to remain positive and we must focus on all of the accomplishments that we have completed in our days. If we are constantly carrying around a list of items that we haven't completed yet, we will always feel distressed as if we are not working hard enough to get everything done. As we talked about in Chapter One, if we feel overwhelmed by time constraints our bodies will react to that. Our bodies will move slower and our minds will cause us to unconsciously procrastinate to avoid plucking away at the work we must get done within our schedule. It is one of the basic principles of time management; we must feel good about ourselves and about our ability to manage time if we are to be efficient in managing it.

We have had many sales professionals come to us and say that they do not need to write out a list each day because their list is in their head. Take it from two people that have tried that method of time management, it does not work. Some of you will be very good at getting most of your tasks completed each day, but you are spending more time throughout your day in the planning process where you are figuring out what item on your schedule needs to get done next. Furthermore, when we ask sales professionals that practice this method of time management if they have ever simply forgotten to do something on their list, the answer is inevitably YES. By having a written list you will save time in your planning process and you will decrease the likelihood of forgetting something important.

Why do we suggest you take no more then 30 seconds at preparing your Quick List each morning? The fact of the matter is, we could all probably spend three hours coming up with lists of things we would like to do in our day. However, by spending too much time on your task list, you eat up valuable time in your day and you end up with a list which is inefficient and unmanageable because it is not a list of the most important items you need to get done and because you end up with a list that leaves you feeling overwhelmed about time causing you to have a physical or mental slowdown which then snowballs into additional time management issues.

The key is to so spend thirty seconds every morning writing your Quick List for the day. You can add to it throughout the day as needed so do not be concerned if it is not 100% accurate. Include any appointments you have throughout the day on your list. We think it is important to have certain routines you complete every day to further your business success. Since we own a real estate company and mortgage company we feel it is important to make contact with ten recruitable or potential new agents each and every day. We also feel it is important to each send out five personal note cards to business associates every day. Therefore, those two tasks are always first on our daily Quick List. Your Quick List should include a mix of some very important tasks for the day, but also some of the little errands that you need to complete.

Once you have taken your thirty seconds to do your Quick List for the day, then at the top of your Quick List write in your two or three Hit List items you are going to accomplish during the week. When you study your weekly Hit List, look to see if there is one item you could add to your daily Quick List which would help you work toward your goal of completing that Hit List task by weeks end.

The Real Estate Playbook Series

Here is a sample 30 second Quick List:

Monday Morning Quick List

Hit List
- Prune Shrubs
- Book a vacation

Quick List
- Make 10 Calls to Potential Buyers or Sellers
- Send out 5 notecards
- Call Michelle back to answer questions.
- Listing appointment with Joe at 10:30.
- Buyer consultation with Nancy at 12:30
- Make two expired packages.
- Pick up a prescription at the pharmacy
- Food shopping
- Send out my weekly email newsletter
- Call Sheryl to confirm for Saturday night
- Order new business cards
- Call Kris to wish her a happy birthday
- Prepare a flyer to be mailed to database next week
- Return four client calls from last evening
- Send email to Brad to thank him for the referral
- Call three landscapers for price on pruning (this is to work toward completion of Hit List task)
- Call three travel agents for vacation quotes (this is to work toward completion of Hit List task)

The first thing we should mention about this list is that you shouldn't plan on listing everything that you plan on completing throughout your day. There will be dozens of other tasks which get co-mingled into the day. The second is that this list is lucid. You will add to it as the day moves forward and you will cross items off as they get completed. The principle reason for having the list at all is to maintain some control over time throughout the day. We all get thrown off course throughout our day by many outside influences. When we are thrown off course we need to recognize that we are off course so that we can grab our Quick List and get right back on track.

We mentioned earlier that our lists are written onto one or two sticky notes each day. The reason we use the sticky notes is because we stick our lists on our computer monitors so they are within our peripheral vision all day. If we leave the office we bring our lists and stick them on the steering wheel or dashboard of our vehicles. Our lists are mobile because we know we will be knocked off our schedules all day long, even in the car, so we want our sticky notes, or our little time maps, to get back on course quickly and efficiently. Incidentally, we always label our lists as well as either "Stacey's List" or "Andy's List". On more then one occasion our lists have gotten mixed into a pile of papers given to the receptionist or even ended up at the bottom of a co-worker's shoe. When someone finds one of our lists, they know where it belongs and we normally get it back. Therefore, always make sure to put a heading on your list so that it will find its way back to you if it gets lost.

Throughout the next two chapters we will be delving more into how these lists relate to delegation of tasks and time blocking. For now it is important to just get into the habit of making the weekly Hit List on Sunday nights and then the Quick Lists each and every morning.

Some of you are wondering whether you should do the Quick Lists on Saturdays and Sundays. There are many weekends that we do not work at the office, however our Quick Lists have been useful in helping us enjoy more productive weekends. We used to have this pandemic where we would go to work every Monday feeling like we had accomplished very little all weekend. We could not figure out where our time was going or why we felt so unfulfilled when it came to our personal time. This is a basic time management problem. Although time management is usually associated with our businesses, it is an issue that is just as important in our personal lives. We feel it is crucial to have Quick Lists on the weekends. We both enjoy making Quick Lists on Saturday and Sunday mornings. These lists look a little different then our weekday Quick Lists, but they have enabled us to manage a more well rounded life. Here is a sample of a Saturday morning Quick List:

Saturday Morning Quick List

Hit List
- Prune Shrubs
- Book a vacation

- Take cat to the vet
- Buy a new hair dryer
- Go to Barnes and Noble to check out new best sellers
- Pick up black pumps for Saturday night wedding
- Go to movie with niece and nephew
- Get birthday present for mom
- Start reading new book
- Try out new coffee place in downtown
- Go over the travel brochures

Our weekend Quick Lists are essential for making sure we have a great weekend. Again, you do not have to list every little task you are going to complete. There will likely be many additional items you will accomplish throughout your weekend, but you should at a minimum list a few key items you would like to complete. You can be confident that something will come along and steal away your time even on Saturdays and Sundays. We want you to be able to grab your list and take charge of your weekend when that happens.

Once you begin practicing your new time management skills you will finish each day with a sense of accomplishment. Furthermore, you will find yourself regularly finishing out each week having completed many of your Hit List items as well. The most important key to time management is feeling good about control over your time. When you regularly maintain that control, you will feel positive and upbeat when you start each day and you will finish each day with a sense of satisfaction and accomplishment.

> **Tip:** Try Hit Listing and Quick Listing today! This is the map to your day. You will inevitably get knocked off your schedule every day. By having your Quick List ready, you will always get back on track in the quickest and most efficient manner possible.

Chapter 5
Delegate Your Plate

Hopefully by this point you have tried out the process of Hit Listing and Quick Listing your days. Writing a list each morning seems like such a simple step and that is probably why so many people just do not do it. These lists serve two very important functions in managing of our time. The first is that they serve to keep us on schedule throughout the day. When we are interrupted by phone calls, co-workers, or problems that pop up, it is sometimes very easy to lose focus on what our goals for the day are and often this causes us to lose an entire day. If you keep your Quick List by your side all day you will constantly be reminded of what it is you planned for, enabling you to remain focused and in control. That is why even if you stopped reading this book at the end of the last chapter and only took away from it the importance of a daily list, you would be well on your way to conquering most of your time management problems. This chapter will focus on how we can further expand upon our Hit Lists and Quick Lists in order to maximize time efficiency throughout the day using the process of delegation.

Delegation is simply the process of assigning certain tasks to others. In the following chapter we will learn how to prioritize those tasks which we have left on our own plate. Prioritization is the process of arranging in the order of importance. What is important to note is that your Quick List is composed in only 30 seconds each morning. The significance of that is that probably everything on the list is pretty important since these are the first things you think about doing when making the list. Our goal is to help you complete everything on your Quick List each day as well as your Hit List each week. In order to get to that point, it is important to study your list and figure out how you are going to conquer it.

Before spending any time on prioritizing your list each day, we will first spend a moment determining what can be delegated to someone else. Delegation of tasks sounds simple, but for many of us, it is extremely difficult. The process of delegating tasks is an art form and upon practicing it daily, you will reap tremendous rewards. Not only will you maximize your time each day, leading you to have more time to earn income, spend time with family, golf, vacation, or do whatever you would like, you will also reap benefits with the people to whom you are delegating. The biggest reward you can pay someone is trust. If you start giving your assistant or receptionist tasks to complete, you are telling them you trust them. Building trust serves to motivate employees to take on more responsibility.

Andy's one of those people that has a hard time delegating. He has the mentality that he can do everything better himself. He does not trust that someone can do the task as good as he can do it himself. However, without learning the ability to delegate, he would never have been able to move forward in business and his personal life at the same rate he has been able to by utilizing his delegation skills. We are all on a level playing field when it comes to time. Each and every one of us is given twenty four hours in a day. If there were no possibilities for getting more time then we would live in a very different world. True entrepreneurs have found a way to get more then twenty four hours in their day and that is through delegation. By allowing others to complete certain tasks on your behalf you are, in a sense buying more time in your day. You expand your time by getting double or triple the number of hours than everyone else has.

Extremely wealthy individuals are usually extremely good at delegation. The reason for this is that they figure out what skill they possess that earns them the best return on time. In other words, they know what the highest and best use of their time is. For example, with most real estate agents, the highest and best use of time is showing houses, listing homes, and prospecting for new business. That is when they are earning income. For loan originators the highest and best use of work time is writing loan applications and prospecting for business. Those who excel in their businesses understand that they must spend a majority of their work day doing these highest and best use tasks so that they are always in a state of earning money during work time. They have the ability to manage their time by handing over tasks to others that, even though they are capable of completing on their own, thereby enabling them to concentrate on their highest and best use tasks.

We have worked closely with top real estate agents and mortgage professionals for years and usually before we demonstrate to them the benefits of delegation, they have this notion engrained into them that they must do everything on their own. We have seen hundreds of real estate agents preparing their own contracts, doing database entry, preparing mailings, and an entire myriad of projects that could easily be passed on to someone else. As well, we have seen loan originators chasing conditions, calling borrowers for insurance binders, and scheduling closings with the title company. All of these are important to their jobs, but it is not important that they individually complete these tasks. These are easily delegated to others.

I know that if I do it myself it will be done right and I'd just rather have control over my own business. That is the objection we normally hear from agents and loan originators. This mentality must change if you are ever to be a top selling agent or loan originator. You cannot close $30 million in real estate transactions or $80 million in mortgage loans if you are in control of the entire process. It is impossible. You will be drained of time, and both your work and home life will suffer. We have seen it happen time and time again. Sales professionals that try to reach super-star status without delegating end up losing control of their time. They live unbalanced lives. They get little time for their families, their partners, or themselves. Over time, resentment builds to the point that they are no longer willing to sacrifice all of their time in return for financial well being. Many end up so burned out that they turn to other careers. With proper delegation skills you will buy yourself plenty of extra time throughout your days so that you will earn financial rewards greater then you could ever have imagined while still having plenty of time to concentrate on other areas of your life.

I can not afford to hire someone so I can not delegate my tasks. This is another excuse we hear from sales professionals too often. The fact is, most of us can not afford NOT to hire someone to delegate to. Before hiring an assistant to help you with your business, see if there are resources within your office that you are already paying for that you can utilize. In many real estate offices there are administrators who will help with your mailings, database entry, and contract preparation. Most offices have such people and often times these staff members are under utilized. If you have this kind of help at your office, use it.

Even if your office does not have an administrator or receptionist to whom you can delegate, we are here to tell you, you can afford to hire someone to assist you. We do not know how much money you have or how much you earn regularly, but that information is of little significance. What you have to look at is how much you are worth on an hourly basis. The easiest way to explain this is by example. Let's take a look at one of the agents that works in our real estate firm. She earned approximately $70,000 last year in her pocket after her commission split. She was terrible with time management. She relied on nobody. She scheduled her own appointments; maintained her database; prepared and mailed her own prospecting flyers each month; prepared contracts; called for feedback on her listings; attended every closing; went to home inspections; and anything else that was required of her. She depended on nobody. Does that sound like you? A majority of real estate agents and originators work just like this.

After sitting with this agent and studying her time and how much of it was spent working we figured she was working approximately sixty hours per week. If you divide the $70,000 by 52 weeks in a year and then sixty hours a week, she was making $22.43 per hour during her day. Ironically, she had come from the high-tech industry where she was earning $25 per hour, so she had taken a pay cut without even realizing it. Not to mention the fact that she was losing precious time with her family and spouse causing friction at home. Anyway, we sat down and made a list of everything she did on a daily basis as part of her job. Here is what her list looked like:

- Schedule showings
- Prepare new marketing materials
- Get mailings out
- Send personal note cards to sphere of influence
- Visit potential clients
- Show homes to potential clients
- Go out and give listing presentations
- Prepare purchase contracts
- Input new listings into Multiple Listing Service

- Prepare pre-listing packages to deliver to client before listing presentation
- Update listings on Craigslist and other sites
- Send out email drip campaigns
- Call other agents for feedback on showings
- Coordinate closings
- Visit expired listings and For Sale By Owner properties
- Attend home inspections
- Hold broker open houses
- Hold client open houses
- Go to social events and mixers
- Order signs to be put up on properties
- Change sign riders each week on houses
- Prepare advertising materials
- Give sellers a weekly feedback report on their listings
- Take photographs of the homes
- Prepare visual tours
- Buy closing gifts

This list does not even come close to documenting every task that a real estate agent completes on a daily basis, but this is the list she came up with. So, we asked the agent to give us the three items from this list which represented the heart and soul of her job. We asked her which three key items contributed the most to her ability to earn $70,000. These are the three items she selected:

- Visit potential clients
- Show homes to potential buyers
- Go out and give listing presentations

We then asked the agent how many hours each week were spent just doing these three tasks. She estimated fifteen hours a week. In essence, this real estate agent was telling us that the $70,000 she earned the year before was really earned in fifteen hours a week because it was these fifteen hours that were crucial to her business success. The other forty five hours each week were spent *preparing* for the fifteen hours where she would use her real talent to make money. Looking at it in this light, we showed her that her actual hourly wage was not $22.43 per hour but was $89.74 per hour. If she spent forty hours per week completing income generating tasks then she would increase her income by 2.5 times and gain twenty hours per week in her schedule. The real estate agent was astounded when she looked at the numbers. She was still skeptical though.

I can not find someone to do the other parts of my job because they are just as important as visiting clients, showing homes to buyers and going out to give listing presentations. It would be impossible to find someone who could do all of the other things I do. This was her initial reaction. So, we went through her list of job duties again and we asked her to visualize herself running her own company and having one full time person who was in the office forty hours a week. We asked her to visualize a real top notch assistant. It had to be somebody who was on the ball and always ready to go the extra mile. We asked her to then place a star next to each task that this assistant could do for her:

- Schedule showings   *
- Prepare new marketing materials   *
- Get mailings out   *
- Send personal note cards to sphere of influence
- Visit potential clients
- Show homes to potential clients

Playbook of HEALTHY TIME MANAGEMENT

- Go out and give listing presentations
- Prepare purchase contracts *
- Input new listings into Multiple Listing Service *
- Prepare pre-listing packages to deliver to client before listing presentation *
- Update listings on Craigslist and other sites *
- Send out email drip campaigns *
- Call other agents for feedback on showings *
- Coordinate closings *
- Visit expired listings and For Sale By Owner properties
- Attend home inspections *
- Hold broker open houses *
- Hold client open houses *
- Go to social events and mixers
- Order signs to be put up on properties *
- Change sign riders each week on houses *
- Prepare advertising materials *
- Give sellers a weekly feedback report on their listings *
- Take photographs of the homes *
- Prepare visual tours *
- Buy closing gifts *

This exercise really enabled her to open her eyes and see that if she continued on her current time management path she had no opportunity to increase her income and she would slowly lose relationships with her family, which was her support network. Her current path was one of eventual self destruction.

I can see how I could benefit by having an assistant but I just do not have the money right now to afford one. She was failing to see that she had just given herself a raise from $70,000 to over $180,000 if she managed her time correctly. Eventually, we convinced her to put an advertisement for a personal assistant on Craigslist. We advised her to advertise that it was a commission job based on production. The figure that she felt comfortable paying an assistant was 15% of her commissions earned each month. Within a couple of weeks this agent ended up hiring someone who had been a real estate agent at one time and who had left the business because it was causing strife at home with the long hours and unpredictable schedule. The new assistant loved the idea of being in the real estate industry while having the ability to maintain a forty hour work schedule. In her first full year of utilizing a sales assistant, this agent went from $70,000 in commissions to $210,000 in commissions. She had no problem paying her assistant $31,500. Not only that, to this day, that agent leaves the office at five o'clock and takes every Sunday off to be with her family. Now that is a time management success story!

Just as hiring a great assistant can lead to a huge boost in available time and a nice raise, the same can be true by partnering up with someone. Both in real estate and mortgage sales, we have seen many great success stories born by partnerships. When prospecting for a good partner in the business, look for someone who is strong in the areas that you are weak. For example, we too are delegation success stories. Without our ability to compliment each other in the delegation of tasks, we would never have been able to run multiple companies, nor even write this time management book! At the beginning of each joint venture we delve into, the two of us sit down and write out a list of what we will each contribute. We know each others strong points as well as weaknesses and we use that as a guide to delegate work amongst one another.

Incidentally, it is just as important to delegate tasks in your personal life. If you are spending four hours a week cleaning, and your time is worth more than the cost of hiring someone to help you with that task, then doesn't it make sense to just hire someone? When we properly manage our time we are able to balance our lives in such a way that we can balance our time between earning a great living and enjoying it. For example, we have a real estate agent friend that hates cooking. She used to gruel over what she would make her family for dinner each week. She would spend so much time planning and going back and forth to the food store that the task just became a chore. She felt tremendous guilt at the thought of not giving her kids a good meal each night and it ended up costing her hours of lost time worrying. One day, she met a woman in line at the grocery store. The woman had a daughter that was about the same age as her own daughter so they started talking. The woman was complaining how hard it was to make small meals since it was only her and her daughter she was feeding. She said how she loved to cook and it was her way of relieving all of the stress when she got home. Well, this agent saw an opportunity and seized it. She asked the woman if she would be interested in selling her leftovers. It turned out that they struck up a friendly agreement where the woman would cook extra large meals each night, keep some for her and her daughter and then package up the rest in containers for our friend. It was a win-win all around. The single mother was pleased with a little extra income for doing something she loved and our agent was ecstatic to be able to offer her family a home cooked meal every night. Our agent delegated a task that she did not enjoy doing giving her more free time to do the things she liked. Another time management success story!

    Maybe you are not ready just yet to retain someone to help you with cooking or cleaning. Even so, there are other ways to save time by delegation. For example, do you utilize the dry cleaning service that will pick up and deliver at your home or office? Do you pay extra when you order lunch to have them deliver to your office? These services cost extra. We know this. However, if you apply the principles we just learned, you will see that it actually costs you much less then if you were to do these tasks yourself.

The point is that there are opportunities to save time both in the personal and business portions of our lives. Every time you seize an opportunity to delegate something you end up gaining additional time in your day.

One caveat we would like to mention is that if you are not earning the income you would like to be earning in your real estate sales or mortgage origination job, it might not come down to a time management issue. It might be that you do not like doing the core work responsibilities that lead to income generation. For example, our agent that we mentioned earlier pinpointed visiting potential clients, showing homes to potential buyers, and going out to give listing presentations were her core income producing activities. If she did not enjoy doing these three tasks each day, then even with the help of an assistant, she would not be able to increase her earning potential. By studying your time closely you will be able to figure out what it is you like to do. If it is not visiting clients, showing homes, and doing listing presentations, it is not the end of the world. Utilize this information and partner up with another sales person in your office who likes to do the things that you do not. Look around your office. It is full of agents with time management issues. Everyone will have different areas of the job they like and do not like. Team up with someone who is your opposite and you will both reap financial rewards.

So now, hopefully we have convinced you on the importance of delegation. Now it is time to review your Quick List and Hit List to see what can be delegated each day. The art of delegation takes practice. Many of us are programmed to do everything ourselves since many of us think of giving work to others as a weakness. In fact, the opposite is true. As we have learned earlier in this book, we have a greater ability to seize control of our schedules and we are able to live more balanced lives when we delegate properly. How do we start the process of delegating?

Look at your Quick List for the day. Let's use the one we put together earlier as an example.

Monday Morning Quick List

Hit List
- Prune Shrubs
- Book a Vacation

Quick List
- Make 10 Calls to Potential Buyers or Sellers
- Send out 5 notecards
- Call Michelle back to answer questions.
- Listing appointment with Joe at 10:30.
- Buyer consultation with Nancy at 12:30
- Make two expired packages.
- Pick up a prescription at the pharmacy
- Food shopping
- Send out my weekly email newsletter
- Call Sheryl to confirm for Saturday night
- Order new business cards
- Call Kris to wish her a happy birthday
- Prepare a flyer to be mailed to database next week
- Return four client calls from last evening
- Send email to Brad to thank him for the referral
- Call three landscapers for price on pruning
- Call three travel agents for vacation quotes

Take out your Quick List and go through it to pick out the items you could delegate to someone else. For example, if you do not have a personal assistant yet, there are probably certain tasks that your administrator could do. Is there anything on your list you could delegate to your spouse or partner? What about your kids?

We had an agent that had a "Movie and Mailing" night every Sunday evening with her kids. Her kids would help her stick labels on her weekly postcard mailings while they enjoyed a movie at their home. Whenever that agent received a new client from her mailing she would have a special dinner celebration with the kids so that they could share in the excitement of new business opportunities. If that client ended up closing on a sale the agent would give a 10% referral check which was split between her two kids. She taught them how to set aside a portion of that check for charity, a portion for savings, and then each would get spending money to buy something special for themselves. Think about all of the life lessons this agent was teaching her kids all while delegating some of her workload to her kids!

If you have trouble finding items on your Quick List to delegate, we urge you to find a buddy to help you. After spending decades learning to depend only upon ourselves, it can be very difficult to see areas where delegation is possible. However, with practice, you will learn that there are not many tasks that can not be delegated. Once you have reviewed your list, put a star next to the items you are going to delegate. Then write in who you are going to delegate to. For example:

Monday Morning Quick List

Hit List
- Prune Shrubs
- Book a Vacation

Quick List
- Make 10 Calls to Potential Buyers or Sellers
- Send out 5 notecards
- Call Michelle back to answer questions.

- Listing appointment with Joe at 10:30.
- Buyer consultation with Nancy at 12:30
- Make two expired packages * (assistant)
- Pick up a prescription at the pharmacy * (spouse/partner)
- Food shopping * (spouse/partner)
- Send out my weekly email newsletter * (receptionist)
- Call Sheryl to confirm for Saturday night * (receptionist)
- Order new business cards * (assistant)
- Call Kris to wish her a happy birthday
- Prepare a flyer to be mailed to database next week * (assistant)
- Return four client calls from last evening
- Send email to Brad to thank him for the referral * (assistant)
- Call three landscapers for price on pruning * (spouse/partner)
- Call three travel agents for vacation quotes * (spouse/partner)

We have seventeen items on this Quick List. We are going to delegate about half of those items. In this example, it saves two to three hours of valuable time. Throughout your day you will want to take a moment here and there to follow up to make sure the items you have delegated have been completed.

You will soon learn which people are the best to delegate to and which ones are not. This is important if you have or are hiring an assistant to help you with your time management. You do not want to have an assistant that requires constant follow up. If you find that you are always reminding the assistant to complete certain tasks then that person is not a good assistant. You want to work with someone that needs no hand holding and you know for certain that if you have asked for something to be completed, it will be completed.

Throughout your day you should cross out the items as you complete them. This will help you stay focused on the tasks at hand, leaving you with a sense of accomplishment which will give you the positive encouragement you need to stay on track all day. As well, you will probably add tasks as your day goes on. It is important to always ask yourself whether the task can be delegated. If so, just as soon as you add the task to your list, you should determine to whom you will delegate and then do so.

Finally, we feel this goes without saying, but there are certain tasks that just can not be delegated. You can not delegate a phone call to wish someone a happy birthday. We each write five personal notes per day, and they come from the heart. That task cannot be delegated. Although many times an assistant can write notes to business associates for you, if it is coming from the heart, it cannot be delegated. If you start delegating too much, such as birthday wishes, or get well calls to a fellow friend or associate, your co-workers and friends will interpret that as your being fake and uncaring. Although it is likely not your intention, it could be perceived in that fashion. Therefore, be careful in what you delegate.

Tomorrow try your hand at some delegation. Take your Quick List and delegate as much as possible. If you are having a hard time with it, give your list to a friend or family member and let them help you through the delegation process. Do not forget to follow up throughout the day to make sure the people to whom you have delegated are getting the job done. Try it out for a week or two and then determine if you need someone to whom you may delegate consistently. Use the formula from the beginning of this chapter to determine how much your earning potential would increase if you had a personal assistant. Are you willing to give up 10% of your income in return for a 40%, 50% or 60% return? If so, it is time to start interviewing!

Within minutes every morning you will now be writing yourself Quick Lists and then delegating as much of the duties as possible. The next step is determining how to go about conquering the day by completing the non-delegated tasks on your Quick List which is all a matter of proper prioritization.

> **Tip:** Tomorrow try your hand at some delegation. Take your Quick List and delegate as much as possible. If you are having a hard time with it, give your list to a friend or family member and let them help you through the delegation process.

CHAPTER 6
PRIORITIZING... EASY AS 1, 2, 3!

We told you earlier that when you are preparing your Quick List every morning you should write down everything you must complete throughout the day. The result is that you have a list of major tasks which must be completed, and then a handful of smaller tasks which you would like to complete. Since some of our daily responsibilities are more important then others, it is important to complete the list in some type of order.

If you are not currently structuring your life by using a time management system you might get stuck in the trap of saving some of the more difficult daily responsibilities for last. When we have a long list of errands to complete throughout the day it is easy to pick off the easier items first. Maybe you have two or three big ticket items that you must accomplish by days end and then you have twenty little chores which you would really like to complete, but these items are not so important that they could not wait for another time. It is pretty tempting to do the twenty little chores and save the rest for later. Many of us are procrastinators by nature and we will put off the difficult work until later.

This book is going to ask you to take a completely different approach to prioritization of your schedule. First we will learn how to prioritize the Quick Lists in an efficient and time saving manner so that you will feel confident and adept at the end of each day. Then, in the following chapter we will take this prioritization process one step further by learning how to prioritize your entire life through a process known as time-blocking. For now, we will start with your Quick List.

Take your Quick List for the day and determine what items are left on your plate. In other words what has not been delegated. If it is easier for you, take a second and write out two lists, one with the items you have delegated, so that you know to check on the status of those items throughout the day. The second list is comprised of items you are going to personally tackle throughout the day. Put a number one next to the items which are an absolute priority. This would be something that must be completed today, no matter what. For example, if you have scheduled an appointment with a client, that is something that must get completed by days end. Next, put a number two next to those items from your list that are difficult or time consuming, but it would not be the end of the world if that item were not completed by days end. Finally, put a number three next to those items that are super easy or take little time and it would not be a big deal if it were not completed. Here is a reference chart for you:

1's = Absolute Priority
2's = Difficult and/or time consuming but not a priority.
3's = Easy and/or take little time and not a priority

This is an extremely basic prioritization schedule. Some time management books will tell you to numerically list the order in which you will complete your work list from 1-10. We do not subscribe to that method only because time is so lucid. You are going to run into obstacles which will take away time. You are also going to be adding items to your list throughout the day. By using this simple 1,2,3 approach you will be able to easily add tasks to your schedule and, after determining whether the task may be delegated, you will be able to assign a priority number to it.

Here is an example of how you might prioritize the list we have been working off of.

Monday Morning Quick List

Hit List
- Prune Shrubs - 3
- Book a vacation - 3

Quick List
- Make 10 Calls to Potential Buyers or Sellers   - 2
- Send out 5 notecards   - 2
- Call Michelle back to answer questions. -1
- Listing appointment with Joe at 10:30. - 1
- Buyer consultation with Nancy at 12:30 - 1
- Make two expired packages * (assistant)
- Pick up a prescription at the pharmacy * (spouse/partner)
- Food shopping * (spouse/partner)
- Send out my weekly email newsletter * (receptionist)
- Call Sheryl to confirm for Saturday night * (receptionist)
- Order new business cards * (assistant)
- Call Kris to wish her a happy birthday -1
- Prepare a flyer to be mailed to database next week * (assistant)

- Return four client calls from last evening -1
- Send email to Brad to thank him for the referral * (assistant)
- Call three landscapers for price on pruning * (spouse/partner)
- Call three travel agents for vacation quotes * (spouse/partner)

There are a couple of things you should note here. First, when we say that 2's and 3's are not a priority, that certainly does not mean that these are not priorities in your every day life. Your Quick List was composed in 30 seconds at the beginning of your morning. These are the items that were first and foremost in your brain when you wrote your list. Basically, the fact that something even made the Quick List signifies that it was a priority. The goal is to get you to a point where every single event listed on your Quick List each day and Hit List each week gets completed. Therefore, when we reference the word priority when it comes to the 1,2,3 list, it only means it is a task which should be completed earlier in time then everything else on the list.

You should take notice of the fact that we did not prioritize anything that has been delegated. Your job will be to follow up on the tasks you have delegated to make sure they get completed, but since you will not be completing those items, there is no reason to prioritize them.

Now that you have prioritized your work day, it is time to start conquering it. You will work through your day by always starting with the 1's. You have to finish the 1's each day. If you get thrown off schedule by something, you will always go back to your Quick List and you will always search for the 1's. It is important to tackle the 1's first because normally, those items are more time consuming and represent an important role in your work or personal life. We all have the most amount of energy when we wake up every morning. As time ticks by, and as day turns to night, our energy fades. That is one of the principal reasons you should work on the important matters first. With energy and vigor you will complete those important items effortlessly.

It is also important to maintain a positive attitude throughout the day. Unless you are a real grouch, you probably wake up each day with a pretty good attitude. That will be enhanced even further as you gain control of your time. Isn't it much easier to get work completed when you feel good about life? Since it is likely that we will hit bumps in the road throughout the day which may decrease our mood or outlook, it is important to get the important items done early. If you save an important task for early afternoon and by that time you have had to put out three early morning fires, you are not going to accomplish that task with the same enthusiasm you would have earlier. In turn, you end up wasting time. Conversely, if you have completed all of your 1's by lunch time, you will be moving into the afternoon hours with the same positive attitude and excitement you had earlier in the morning.

As you complete tasks throughout each day, look for areas where you can double up and accomplish two tasks simultaneously. We will learn how to hone in on this skill in the chapter on multi-tasking. However, as you are practicing your prioritization skills, make sure to start looking for items from your list that can be conquered at the same time. Also, do not forget to take time to follow up on the delegated tasks. You will want to make sure those items get finished as well. As you complete each item on the list, put a line through it. Do not scribble it out completely because the most important part of your day is tallying up your accomplishments.

One of the best parts of time managing your day will be the late afternoon or early evening where you take out a piece of paper and write out your accomplishments. At the top of the page write in the date and then write ACCOMPLISHMENTS. Then, go about listing everything you completed that day. If it was something you completed from your Quick List or Hit List, write it down. If it was something that never made your list, but you feel good about getting it done, write it down. If it was a task you delegated, still put it on your Accomplishments List but put a little star next to that item. When your Accomplishments List is complete, hang it somewhere so you can see it for the rest of the night and so you see it as you are getting ready the next morning. Hang it on your refrigerator, your bathroom mirror, or put it on your night stand. You will conclude each night and start each morning by focusing on all of the things you have completed instead of focusing on what you haven't. This will put you in the perfect state of mind for moving into the next day with the positive mental attitude which is necessary for planning and implementing the next day's schedule.

What about items that did not get completed? Once you have a systemized approach to managing your day, you will probably have one spot where you sit and write your Quick List each morning. If so, write down anything that you might want to add to the Quick List tomorrow and leave it in that spot. Mentally, you should let go of those items that did not get done. If you find yourself focusing on the uncompleted items from your list just say to yourself repeatedly, "I have plenty of time to get those things done on another day. I am so excited that I got so much done today!"

> **Tip:** Each day make a list of your Accomplishments and hang it somewhere so that you may see it for the entire evening. Too often we focus on all that we did not complete instead of what we did, and this feeling of being unfulfilled is counteractive to the positive attitude which is necessary for proper time management.

Chapter 7
Time Blocking – Be Your Own Client

We have found that this is one of the most difficult areas of time management for real estate agents, mortgage originators, and sales professionals in general. Much of this stems from the fact that we all rely on commissions. We harbor this feeling that if someone calls and wants to look at homes or if someone needs a mortgage, everything in the world must come to a halt because we do not want to risk the possibility of losing that client which could lead to our next paycheck. This way of thinking is a time management nightmare and it is not the most efficient way to run a business. In fact, this mentality can crush a career.

As successful sales professionals, a large portion of our time must be spent with a systemized approach to lead generation so that referrals are constantly coming in. That means that we have to make sure that our lead generation tasks are an ongoing part of our weekly work cycle. When we are racing around at the whim of our buyers, sellers, and borrowers, many of us lose focus on the essential lead generation part of our business. Lead generation is our oxygen. If we deprive our business of this for any length of time, it will die. We have seen so many agents and loan originators let their careers be dictated at the whim of the next buyer, borrower, or seller to the point that it is virtually impossible to manage time which means every aspect of their career and personal lives suffer. These agents or loan officers stop doing lead generation. They also stop setting aside personal, family, and relationship time. They basically squeeze in a little bit of these other parts of their lives when they can. We are here to tell you that this is no way to run a business and it is certainly no way to live! We must **time block** our way to successful careers as well as happy and fulfilling lives.

So, what is time blocking. Time blocking is an exercise where you review your calendar each day and you set aside certain increments of time in order to accomplish certain goals. Do you remember the exercise we did earlier in the book where we divided up our week and made time for all of the important events in our lives? Here was the one that we did earlier:

WEEKLY SCHEDULE

	SUN	MON	TUES	WED	THURS	FRI	SAT
5:00 AM		Spiritual	Spiritual	Spiritual	Spiritual	Spiritual	Spiritual
6:00 AM	Household						
7:00 AM	Household	Work	Work	Work	Work	Work	Work
8:00 AM	Household	Work	Work	Work	Work	Work	Work
9:00 AM	Household	Work	Work	Work	Work	Work	Work
10:00 AM	Household	Work	Work	Work	Work	Work	Work
11:00 AM	Household	Work	Work	Work	Work	Work	Family
12:00 PM	Relationship	Me	Me	Me	Me	Me	Family
1:00 PM	Relationship	Work	Work	Work	Work	Work	Family
2:00 PM	Relationship	Work	Work	Work	Work	Work	Family
3:00 PM	Relationship	Work	Work	Work	Work	Work	Family
4:00 PM	Relationship	Work	Work	Work	Work	Work	Family
5:00 PM	Relationship	Work	Work	Work	Work	Work	Family
6:00 PM	Relationship	Work	Work	Work	Work	Work	Me
7:00 PM	Relationship	Relationship	Relationship	Relationship	Relationship	Me	Me
8:00 PM		Me	Me	Me	Me		
9:00 PM							

The importance of boxing out time slots for all aspects of our lives was so that we could balance our lives with just the right mix of work time, relationship time, me time, family time, household time, and spiritual time. Without really studying and taking hold of our time, most of us end up leading extremely unbalanced lives. There is an old adage which says, "the squeaky wheel gets the grease." Without getting a grip on our time, then certain aspects of our lives will become the greasy wheel, and will get all of our time. For many, the squeaky wheel is work which causes ones personal life to suffer greatly.

In order to time block your week or month, you first must have a schedule. We prefer the daily schedule which breaks down the entire day by hour. It is important to get used to writing down events in your schedule and blocking out parts of each day to accomplish everything in your life that is important. When blocking time you are going to write down the parts of your day where you will accomplish major tasks while keeping in mind your greater goals which you outlined in a chart similar to the one above. Let's take a look at an example of a weekly schedule.

The Real Estate Playbook Series

Example of weekly schedule

7:00	Breakfast	Breakfast	Breakfast	Breakfast	Breakfast	Breakfast	Breakfast
7:30	Quicklist	Quicklist	Quicklist	Quicklist	Quicklist	Quicklist	Quicklist
8:00	Work on List	Work on List	Women's Council Meet	Work on List	Work on List		Church
8:30	↓	↓	↓	↓	↓	Exercise	↓
9:00	↓	Return Calls/Email	↓	↓	↓	↓	↓
9:30	↓	↓	Work on List	↓	↓		
10:00	Return Calls/Email	Office Meeting	↓	Return Calls/Email	Tour	Vet Appt	
10:30	↓	↓	↓	↓	↓	↓	
11:00		↓	↓		↓		
11:30		↓			↓		
Noon	Lunch	Lunch	Returns Calls/Emails	Lunch	Return Calls/Email		Lunch
12:30 PM			↓		↓		
1:00			Lunch		Lunch	Lunch	Exercise
1:30							↓
2:00	Negotiate Offer - Pete			CMA at 23 Orchard		Show Homes to Welch's	
2:30	↓			↓		↓	
3:00				↓	Time with Kids	↓	
3:30					↓	↓	
4:00		Exercise	Time with Kids	Exercise	↓	Movie with spouse	
4:30	Meet Smiths	Food Shop	↓	↓	↓	↓	↓
5:00	↓	↓	↓	↓	↓	↓	↓
5:30	↓	↓	↓	↓	↓	↓	↓
6:00	Family Dinner	Family Dinner	↓	Family Dinner	↓	↓	
7:00	↓	Boy Scouts	Family Dinner	Movie Night	Family dinner	Dinner Out	
8:00	↓	↓		↓	Family night		Fixlist
9:00	Bed	Bed	Bed	Bed	Bed	Bed	Bed
10:00							
11:00							

Should you be concerned if you haven't time blocked every single block each week? Absolutely not! In fact, it would be practically impossible to do. As sales professionals we do need to be flexible in our schedules, just not so flexible that we no longer have a schedule. There should be plenty of open time throughout the week so that you can work in changes and additions to your time as they are presented. Do not forget, that your Quick List and Hit List will be the thread that sews your schedule together. When you are faced with vacant time slots, take advantage of that time to work on your all important lists. Check in on the items you have delegated, and try to work on your Quick List based on the priority you assigned to each task.

Is it important that the weekly schedule does not exactly match your earlier time management breakdown where you wrote down what areas of your life you would concentrate on each week? No. What is important is that you keep your earlier time map with you while you are time blocking your week. Make sure that you are time blocking not only work, but also family time, me time, spiritual time, and time to work on your relationships.

We have worked with hundreds of very motivated real estate agents and loan originators. Many of them utilized a schedule in some aspects of their business. For example, most of us write down appointments we have with clients. Whether it is instinct or rules of business management that have been engrained in us, we know that it is impolite to miss meetings with others and that such behavior will lead to reduced sales and lower pay checks. Therefore, most of us do not even think twice about making sure that we write down these appointments. What happens when a friend calls and asks if you want to hang out during the same time that you have an appointment with a client? For most of us we just say, "No, I can not hang out at that time because I have an appointment. Let's do it later."

It is always amazing that as sales professionals we are so protective of others time, yet we have no problem giving our own away. When someone calls to book an appointment when you have already scheduled one with another client, we simply let the person know the time has been accounted for and let them select another available time. What happens when you planned on having dinner at 6pm with the family and a client calls out of the blue and wants to go look at your listing on 42 Main Street at 6pm? It is that listing that has been on the market for ninety days without a showing. Your seller is all over you because nobody is looking at the house. What happens to the family dinner? For many agents, it gets postponed, rescheduled, or forgotten about.

I can not risk losing a $500,000 buyer, you might say. Then we ask, what would you do if you had an appointment to show three homes to a client at 6pm? Many of you realize then, that you would inform the new client that you already had an agreement with another client to show homes and you would ask for another convenient time to show the property on Main Street. Why is it that we do not give ourselves or our families the same treatment when it comes to time as our clients? We plead with you to start today. Start time blocking for yourself and for your family. When someone calls and wants an appointment with you when you have already blocked time for yourself or your family, do the same thing you would do if you were meeting another client, just ask them to choose a different time.

Many of you will be completely skeptical that this will work. We are telling you that it does. Maybe an analogy will help. As important as our jobs as real estate agents or loan originators are, most of us would agree that doctors have careers which are even more important. Have you ever been in a position where you felt like you had some sort of medical emergency where you wanted to see your doctor right away. Maybe it was a terribly soar throat. Maybe it was more serious like a lump on the back of your leg. Did you try calling your doctor at seven o'clock on a Saturday night to see if there is any way he or she would meet you that evening. Most of us would not even make that phone call because we already know that our doctor is not interrupting his or her personal time to deal with our crisis at that moment. The same is true for lawyers and accountants. Doctors, lawyers, and accountants are professionals. They set standards for how they will conduct their businesses. They want your business because, when you get right down to it, they are sales professionals just like you and me. They do not make a living unless they have happy clients. They have learned, however, that it is possible to maintain happy clients, and healthy businesses, all while setting boundaries for those clients. As real estate agents and loan originators we must learn to set those boundaries as well, and as we do so, we too will have strong businesses, healthy self esteem, and happy families.

The first key to time blocking is to write down everything you are going to do in a given week. It is vitally important to write down everything work related, as well as family, you, and relationship related. The second key is learning to politely say no. Remember, we must treat ourselves and our families like clients. If someone wants to take up time that we have blocked for our kids, the answer must simply be, "I have already booked an appointment for that time." Then let the client choose another time. The new client will respect the boundaries because they think you are working with another client during that period. To take it one step further, you could even inform your client that 6:00-7:30 is the time you spend with your family and that you never book appointments during this special time unless you have advanced notice. Is there any client that wouldn't respect that response? If there is such a client, maybe it shouldn't be yours.

The last two keys to time blocking are simple steps you can take to make managing your time that much easier. The first is taking control of the conversation when someone is looking to schedule time with you. Do not lose sight of the fact that you are a professional. Many of us will let the client dictate the schedule carte blanche. Instead, when a client calls for a CMA, try this approach, "I have Thursday at 2:00 pm or 5pm available or Saturday any time between 3:00 and 5:00. Which time would work for you?" Now you are in control of the schedule and you are not putting yourself in a position of disclosing what times you can not meet them. In most cases, the client will select one of the options you have selected, only because you have given them no choice. If none of those times will work for the client, then select a couple more times that you have available. You must be the one to remain in control of your schedule.

The final key to time blocking success is to utilize your voicemail for setting standards with your clients. If your phone is ringing for you all day long, you will never get anything accomplished if you answer each call as it comes in. In fact you will be running around all day completing tasks which were dictated by the caller and finding it difficult to get anything done. Does your doctor take calls as they come in all day? Of course not, she has a strict schedule she is adhering to. Instead, pick one or two hours per day when you will return phone calls. So that no client goes too long without a return call, it is best to have time in the morning and afternoon where you will return calls. We are even going to take it one step further. We all have those clients that will call every 15 minutes and leave three messages, like "Hi Stacey, I ran outside to get the paper and wasn't sure if I missed your return phone call so I thought I'd call back." Even worse, we have some clients that are so high maintenance that they'll just call someone else if they do not hear back right away. So that we can work through our schedule without constant interruption from calls, we recommend that you change your voicemail box each morning to let the caller know at which times you will be returning calls. Something like this will work, "It's a GREAT day at Stacey's office today! Today is Friday February 9th and it is going to be a great one. I am sorry I wasn't available to take your call, but please do leave a message. Today, I will be returning calls between 11:00-12:00 and from 3:00-4:30. I look forward to talking to you, so please do not forget to leave a phone number where I will be able to reach you during these times. Have a great day!" Now, this message has decreased the likelihood of a client calling multiple times and it is less likely you will lose a client who is waiting around for a phone call. Sales professionals who become adept at time management do the same exact thing with their email. Many of us receive hundreds of emails each day and sometimes just knowing that messages are piling up can be a distraction. Why not set up an auto-responder that says "Thanks for your email! I really look forward to reading this. I will be returning emails today from 10:30 to 11:00 and from 2:00-3:00. Make it a great day!" Now that is taking charge of time!

Now, are we guaranteeing that you will never lose a client by adopting these steps in order to take charge of your schedule and your time? No. Occasionally you might lose a client. Usually a client that is that time sensitive will have loyalty issues with their real estate agent or loan originator anyway, and is therefore probably not worth your time. What is more likely to happen is that by controlling the management of your time you will become increasingly more productive which will lead to increased business. As well, you will live a much more balanced life when you treat yourself, your family, and your partner just like you would any client.

> **Tip:** One key to effective time management is setting up your voicemail box to let callers know at which times you will be returning phone calls. This way your client will not be waiting around for a call and you will reduce the likelihood that the client will call multiple times trying to reach you.

Chapter 8
Multi-Tasking and Non-Event Planning

If you are getting the hang of Quick Listing, Delegation, Prioritization, and Time-Blocking you are well on your way to taking control of your time. After just one week of practicing these skills you are going to feel like a new person. As you set boundaries at work, your clients and co-workers will gain respect for your time. As you prioritize your family and yourself, you will not start each day with a feeling of guilt or resentment toward your career. In a word, you will feel in control. You will soon find yourself taking back control of your time at the slightest sign that it might be wriggling from your grip. For the remainder of the book we are going to look at several techniques to use in conjunction with the time management skills you have already learned.

Multi-tasking is an ability to execute several tasks at once. Most of us practice this skill every day without even realizing it. Do you read the paper while you eat breakfast? Do you return telephone calls while driving? Do you start preparing your dinner at night while doing other household chores? There are a million examples of multi-tasking in our every day lives. By taking on multiple tasks at one time, we get more accomplished in a shorter amount of time.

We all start multi-tasking the moment we get up in the morning when we begin preparing a mental list of everything we need to get done while at the same time getting read to go to work. If you are good at this type of mental preparation then when you get to the office and start writing your Quick List it only takes about thirty seconds because you already know in advance what is going to be on it.

By recognizing and perfecting your ability to multi-task you will always be looking for ways to save time by doubling on tasks. You must be equally adept at recognizing the times when you are not multi-tasking and then doing something about it. For example, the other day, Andrew was calling his bank to inquire about opening a second checking account. Making the call was something that was on his Quick List for that day. He was on hold for at least ten minutes. He sat at his desk and the speakerphone was on while he was listening to the radio station that was playing the on-hold music. As he sat there, he was thinking about everything he needed to accomplish by days end. Then it occurred to him that he was wasting time. In his mind, since he was calling the bank he was accomplishing a task from his Quick List, but what he did not realize was that there were other things he could do while he was waiting on hold. So, Andy quickly grabbed his Quick List and scanned it.

For the remaining five minutes that he was on hold with his bank he started reading and returning emails. He read six emails and responded to three. Now five minutes in saved time is not a lot of time but what if he did that twelve times throughout an entire day. That would amount to one entire hour of time that he saved in his schedule. That is why it is extremely important to always have your Quick List with you. Remember we told you that our Quick Lists are always on a sticky note and we stick them on our computer monitors or steering wheels when we drive. Now do you see why? There is always something on that list that we can work on if we find a vacant slot in our time schedules. What is important is to realize that sometimes those vacant time slots are not completely vacant, they are merely open enough so that you can double up on tasks.

By the way, it is even possible to multi-task some enjoyment in your life. For example, Stacey really enjoys reading books. She just can not get enough. She reads all kinds of things from business management books to mysteries to classics. Since she can not ever get as much time as she would like to read, you can be sure that there is always a book on tape playing in her car cd player. How much time do you spend in your car each day, going to work, appointments, soccer practice, shopping, or home? If you enjoy reading, why not always make sure you are doing that, even when you are driving!

Another skill we have developed is multi-tasking by making non-events. To us, a non-event is a task to which we spend very little time or energy completing. An example of a non-event might be cleaning the house. Many of us do not enjoy cleaning the house. If you are not a fan of cleaning the house then why not make it a non-event in your time management schedule! Many people spend a half hour a day or three hours on a weekend just cleaning their homes. For many of us that is a dreaded waste of valuable time where we would rather be working or relaxing. By multi-task the entire chore of cleaning the house you can make it into a non-event. The following pages will describe how it is possible to multi-task something into a non-event.

While you are preparing breakfast in the morning, wash dishes or load the dishwasher. While you are watching your favorite program on television at night, fold laundry. Then spend every television commercial vacuuming, sweeping, or washing floors. As soon as the program's back on, get back to relaxing. While you wait for the shower to warm up, put away laundry or clean the bathroom. Dust or do loads of laundry while preparing dinner. In other words, do not make cleaning the house an event on your time schedule. Instead, multi-task the entire event. By making cleaning a non-event in then you do bits and pieces of it while multi-tasking with other items you are doing each day.

We have a friend that has her own spin on making certain tasks non-events. Our friend despises food shopping. We have told her a million times that she should delegate the task to her spouse or even hire one of those home delivery services, but she is stubborn about this particular task because she feels she is the only one who understands exactly what everyone in her household likes to eat and if she were to delegate or hire a food delivery service, they would not get it right. So, since she does not enjoy food shopping, she has compromised. She has a family of four and she food shops once a month. She brings one of her kids with her and they fill two carts full of food that will last for the entire month. Each week she will make stops at the convenience store if they run out of milk or bread. However, because she has reduced food shopping to a task which only gets completed twelve times per year, in her mind, it is really not an event at all. Now that is a time management success story!

Begin today being more deliberate in your multi-tasking. When you find yourself on hold or waiting in line or at an appointment, pull out your Quick List and start working on it. Become efficient at multi-tasking and you will save yourself hours each week in your schedule.

Tip: When Quick Listing each morning highlight tasks which you might be able to complete simultaneously to save time.

CHAPTER 9
THE PACMAN PROBLEM

Remember that game, Pacman. The little round yellow guy that raced around the screen munching up nuggets before the ghosts attacked. Is Pacman a little bit like you, racing through the day trying to gobble up pieces of time before the ghosts come and steal it all away? The most difficult part of time management is that as our businesses, families, and friendships grow so does the potential for losing time. If we learn effective ways to control the people that might steal away pieces of our day, then we will become better at our own time management. This chapter will go through some very effective ways of managing people in order to manage time.

The first tip is to tell people in advance about your commitment to time management. For example, when you hire a new person to work on your team as an assistant, or even when you take on a new client, explain to them that you are not always available to them on a seconds notice. Now, obviously there is a proper way to do this and an improper way. For example, you do not want to tell a new client or new team member that you are extremely busy and that you will get to them when you get to them. Instead, explain to them that you lead an extremely structured day so that you can effectively serve all of your clients and team members. Let them know that since your day is so structured, sometimes you are not available right when that person needs you. However, explain that they should always rest assured that they are never stranded on an island alone and if they just leave you a message by voicemail or email, they can always expect a return phone call within hours. We know this seems like a simple step to take. However, most sales people do not do it. Many become so focused on pleasing the new client or team member at the beginning of the relationship that they forget to set appropriate boundaries. Make it a point to start setting these boundaries right from the beginning and you will notice an immediate difference in how people respect your time. Outsiders will respect your time limitations and can appreciate them if you explain it properly.

By the way, when it comes to explaining time boundaries, we have found that it is just as effective to communicate them within your business as it is outside of your business. Do you have family members or friends that always seem to call you at the wrong time? Rather then avoid their phone calls or get stressed out that they are trying to communicate at inconvenient times, just set the boundaries. Let your friends and family members know that you run a very efficient time schedule and that the reason that you do it is so that you can have more free time with them. Let them know the best times and the best mediums to use when contacting you.

Gottaminute? How many times do you hear that in a day? When you hear that infamous word, *Gottaminute?*, all we can advise you to do is RUN! Everyone knows when someone asks if you Gottaminute?, it is never a minute. Sometimes it is five minutes, an hour, or half a day. Do not let the Gottaminutes? get you! This chapter will explain the steps you must take to eliminate the Gottaminutes? from your life. First, if you are in your office working on a project or trying to get an hour or two of time to concentrate on your Quick List or an important matter, just shut the door! We know what you are thinking. You do not want people to think you are a jerk because your door is shut. *Who cares what they think?* If anyone cares that you have your door shut, it is probably because they want to steal a chunk of your time away for no good reason. If you are at your office with the door shut, it is because you are there to work and get things done. It is not rude to concentrate on efficiently running your business.

We strongly recommend that you spend part of every day in your office with the door shut. Let the administrator or receptionist know that you are unavailable for phone calls during those hours. Do not forget to set up your voicemail box to let people know at which times you will be returning calls. Do not feel guilty for being strict with your time here. No interruptions means no interruptions.

Inevitably, you will always have those people that will knock on the door and try to interrupt your time. Should you let them in your space and take care of their problem? No….absolutely not. This is your time to get things done. When that knock comes on your door and somebody pops their head in with the famous quip, *Gottaminute?*, your answer should be, "No. The reason the door is shut is that I am in the middle of something important and time sensitive. I do have some time that I can call you or you could come back either at 3:00 or 5:00. What time would be better for you?" Most people will be respectful of this answer. They will choose a time spot and you can get back to them later. It is really important that you do not let anyone overstep boundaries. You cannot answer their particular question at that time. If it is a quick two second question and you really feel obliged to answer, let the person know that you are going to be getting up from your desk in 15 minutes to get a coffee and then you will stop by their office to answer the question. Remember, this is about respecting your time boundaries.

If you find that office interruptions are constant even with the door shut, put a friendly sign outside the door. "Power Hour in Session – No Interruptions," is a great way to notify people of your wish to be left in solitude. You can even take this one step further by leaving a sign up sheet with your available times on the door so that people can sign up for a time slot to talk with you. Both the "Power Hour" sign and the sign up sheet are also handy when you are working in a cubicle. Again, you have to be the one to stick to the boundaries when someone comes over and tries to cross them.

One effective method we have seen used for managing time is to remove the chairs from your office. This is great if you find people constantly stopping by your office to chat and you have a difficult time asking them to leave. By removing the chairs, you can be certain most people will not stay for very long because they'll be tired of standing. The downside to this is that you will have to schedule meetings and interviews in a conference room area.

Of course, in the real estate, mortgage, and sales business we are always going to have to meet with people on a one on one basis. Shutting the door to the office or setting up Power Hour signs will always help us get some solitude, but we also need to know how to effectively control our time when we are with people. The best way to do that is to, once again, communicate. If you have a meeting with a client, let them know in advance how long that meeting will take. Set the expectation in advance. If you are meeting with a team member to go over a problem, let them know right when they sit with you that they have your undivided attention for a certain length of time. Most people really appreciate knowing in advance how much time they can expect for the meeting.

There are a few cues you can practice once you notice that it is getting close to the time that the meeting should be ending. First, glance at your watch ten minutes before the meeting should be ending. This will normally give the other party a cue that their time with you is coming to an end. About five minutes before the meeting is over, stand up from your chair. You will probably continue to wrap up the meeting, but standing up will ensure that you are out of the meeting right on time. Also, it is never impolite to let the other party know how much time is left in the meeting so that they can address any other issues before your time together is over.

We should also note that often times it is not people that munch away our time. Sometimes it is other distractions such as television, email, instant messaging, text messaging, etc. Whatever it is that takes your time away, you must eliminate it. If you have a home office and you find that you get caught up listening to the news or watching programs while you are trying to work, then shut the television off or stop working out of your house. If you are at the office with your Power Hour sign on the side of your desk and you keep checking emails every five minutes, then shut your email off. Learn to be disciplined with your time and become adept at recognizing the areas that are taking up your available time.

Finally, when it comes to the Pacman problem, please take a step back and see if maybe you are the ghost taking time away from others. Learn to be respectful of others time and they will be respectful of yours. When an office door is shut, leave it shut. Instead of asking if someone's Gottaminute?, ask them if you can schedule in 5 minutes with them later in the day or the next morning. Set a tone within your office and within your relationships with friends and family which shows how important you think their time is. In return, you will foster relationship with them where they value your time equally.

> **Tip:** Eliminate the Pacman ghosts who are gobbling up your time! The best way to do so is to communicate your time boundaries with team members and clients in advance so that you can give them your undivided attention and loyalty to their needs when you have scheduled a particular time to talk to them.

Chapter 10
Technology and Time

No good time management book can go without a chapter which addresses technology. In fact, technology has is many ways saved us all hundreds of hours per year in time. Many of us are very skeptical to embrace new technology, but when we eventually do, we immediately enjoy the benefits of saved time. What are some ways that technology has saved us time?

One of our biggest time savers is email. With email we are now able to communicate without really communicating. In other words, you can communicate a message to someone while avoiding the long drawn out conversation. What is even more beneficial is the ability to now conduct several conversations simultaneously using email. Most of us are usually holding twenty or more conversations at any one time using our email. As well, we are now able to contact thousands of people in our database without having to sit and lick stamps and stuff envelopes. One press of a button and you have emailed a newsletter to everyone you know, plus some! .

With the new wireless internet cards, agents can easily sit at any open house with a lap top, returning emails and doing property searches while conducting the open house. At one time, we were forced to sit at open houses waiting idol for a potential customer to come through the door. With today's inventions, we can sit there and conduct two hours of fruitful work while we wait. This is multi-tasking at its best.

As we mentioned in the previous chapters, it is important to recognize when there is an opportunity to multi-task. To this day, we stop by open houses and see agents sitting there idol. Shame on them for not taking advantage of their ability to return emails and design flyers or video tours on their lap top at an open house! The excuse will normally be that such technology costs money. Our reply will always be that sitting idol for two hours a weekend and over one hundred hours a year is clearly much more expensive.

Remember the old days of real estate when you had to drive to an office to pick up a key? Today we have lock boxes with e-keys. That saves us hours per week because now we can go right from property to property without having to make arrangements to pick up keys. Our cell phones now come with all of our contact management software and calendars right inside them. We still prefer to make our Hit Lists and Quick Lists on a sticky pad, but many of you will enjoy doing the same exact lists right on your phones. We encourage that! We encourage technology all the way around.

When it comes to new technology, such as text messaging, instant messaging, and new software capabilities we encourage all sales people to embrace it. Sometimes we shy away from new technology because of the time or money it takes to learn them. However, the initial investment needed to learn most new technology pays back tenfold in saved time and money over the years. If a new software program or gadget is introduced to the market, find a class or training program and time block it into your schedule. Learn it! Five hours spent learning something new could end up saving you five hours a week in wasted time. Do not forget that saved time means saved money. Embrace technology!

> **Tip:** Always embrace new technology! It is never too expensive if it saves you hours of time in your daily or weekly schedules. Always go back to basics and calculate the value of your time in dollars. You will then recognize that most technology will actually save you thousands of dollars in saved time.

In Closing

We hope you enjoyed the first book in our Playbook Series. We are committed to helping agents and originators across the country foster flourishing real estate and mortgage careers by sharing everything we have learned from all the bumps and bruises we have encountered in our businesses.

Words to Live By...

If you live in the river you should make friends with the crocodile.

Indian Proverb

You cannot have what you do not want.

John Acosta

Fools take to themselves the respect that is given to their office.

Aesop

Adaptability is not imitation. It means power of resistance and assimilation.

Mahatma Gandhi

The first requisite for success is the ability to apply your physical and mental energies to one problem incessantly without growing weary.

Thomas A. Edison

Whether you think you can or whether you think you can't, you're right!

Henry Ford

Man cannot discover new oceans unless he has the courage to lose sight of the shore.

Andre Gide

The truth of the matter is that you always know the right thing to do. The hard part is doing it.

Norman Schwarzkopf

Winning starts with beginning.

Robert H. Schuller

Act as if what you do makes a difference. It does.

William James

People say to me, "You were a roaring success. How did you do it?" I go back to what my parents taught me. Apply yourself. Get all the education you can, but then, by God, do something. Don't just stand there, make something happen.

Lee Iacocca

The question "Who ought to be boss?" is like as "Who ought to be the tenor in the quartet?" Obviously, the man who can sing tenor.

Henry Ford

In order for the light to shine so brightly, the darkness must be present.

Danny Devito

I had no ambition to make a fortune. Mere money-making has never been my goal, I had an ambition to build.

John D. Rockefeller

Keep away from small people who try to belittle your ambitions. Small people always do that, but the really great make you feel that you, too, can become great.

Mark Twain

Our loyalties must transend our race, our tribe, our class, and our nation; and this means we must develop a world perspective.

Martin Luther King Jr.

In War: Resolution. In Defeat: Defiance. In Victory: Magnanimity. In Peace: Goodwill.

Winston Churchill

The Green Bay Packers never lost a football game. They just ran out of time.

Vince Lombardi

Your mental attitude is someting you can control outright and you must use self-discipline until you create a Positive Mental Attitude -- your mental attitude attracts to you everything that makes you what you are.

Napolean Hill

What happens to a man is less significant than what happens within him.

Louis L. Mann

Any fact facing us is not as important as our attitude toward it, for that determines our success or failure.

Norman Vincent Peale

I don't pay good wages because I have a lot of money; I have a lot of money because I pay good wages.

Robert Bosch

No sale is really complete until the product is worn out, and the customer is satisfied.

L.L. Bean

You can't run a business or anything else on a theory.

Harold S. Geneen

A business that makes nothing but money is a poor kind of business.

Henry Ford

Dreams are the touchtones of our characters.

Henry David Thoreau

Have faith in your dreams and someday your rainbow will come smiling through. No matter how your heart is grieving, if you keep on believing, the dream that you wish will come true.

Cinderella

Now, I say to you today my friends, even though we face the difficulties of today and tomorrow, I still have a dream. It is a dream deeply rooted in the American dream. I have a dream that one day this nation will rise up and live out the true meaning of its creed: -- we hold these truths to be self-evident, that all men are created equal.

Martin Luther King Jr.

You know the world is going crazy when the best rapper is a white guy, the best golfer is a black guy, the tallest guy in the NBA is Chinese, the Swiss hold the America's Cup, France is accusing the U.S. of arrogance, Germany doesn't want to go to war, and the three most powerful men in America are named Bush, Dick, and Colon.

Chris Rock

Don't cry because its over, Smile because it happened!

Dr. Seuss

Imagination is more important than knowledge. For knowledge is limited to all we now know and understand, while imagination embraces the entire world, and all there ever will be to know and understand.

Albert Einstein

Anyone who can be replaced by a machine deserves to be.

Dennis Gunton

Think left and think right and think low and think high. Oh, the thinks you can think up if only you try!

Dr. Seuss

I never hit a shot, not even in practice, without having a very sharp, in-focus picture of it in my head. First I see the ball where I want it to finish, nice and white and sitting up high on the bright green grass. Then the scene quickly changes, and I see the ball going there: its path, trajectory, and shape, even its behavior on landing. Then there is a sort of fade-out, and the next scene shows me making the kind of swing that will turn the previous images into reality.

Jack Nicklaus

There are no such things as limits to growth, because there are no limits to the human capacity for intelligence, imagination, and wonder.

Ronald Reagan

Life is 10% of what happens to me and 90% of how I react to it.

John Maxwell

What lies behind us and what lies before us are tiny matters compared to what lies within us.

Walt Emerson

You were not born a winner, and you were not born a loser. You are what you make yourself be.

Lou Holtz

Obstacles don't have to stop you. If you run into a wall, don't turn around and give up. Figure out how to climb it, go through it, or work around it.

Michael Jordan

We must become the change we want to see.

Mahatma Gandhi

If you judge people, you have no time to love them.

Mother Teresa

It ain't about how hard ya hit. It's about how hard you can get it and keep moving forward. How much you can take and keep moving forward. That's how winning is done! Now if you know what you're worth then go out and get what you're worth.

Rocky Balboa

If you would lift me up you must be on higher ground.

Ralph Waldo Emerson

Never give up, for that is just the place and time that the tide will turn.

Harriet Beecher Stowe

May the sun always shine on your windowpane; May a rainbow be certain to follow each rain; May the hand of a friend always be near you; May God fill your heart with gladness to cheer you.

Irish Blessing

Seek first to understand, then to be understood.
> **Stephen Covey**

Do you want to know who you are? Don't ask. Act! Action will delineate and define you.
> **Thomas Jefferson**

We make way for the man who boldly pushes past us.
> **Christian Nevell Bovee**

It's hard to beat a person who never gives up.
> **Babe Ruth**

I do not think that there is any other quality so essential to success of any kind as the quality of perseverance. It overcomes almost everything, even nature.
> **John D. Rockefeller**

A man is not finished when he's defeated; he's finished when he quits.
> **Richard M. Nixon**

Our greatest weakness lies in giving up. The most certain way to succeed is always to try just one more time.

Thomas A. Edison

I've missed over 9,000 shots in my career. I've lost almost 300 games. 26 times I've been trusted to take the game-winning shot . . . and missed. I've failed over and over and over again in my life. And that is why I succeed.

Michael Jordan

Champions keep playing until they get it right.

Billie Jean King

This I do know beyond any reasonable doubt. Regardless of what you are doing, if you pump long enough, hard enough and enthusiastically enough, sooner or later the effort will bring forth the reward.

Zig Ziglar

When you come to the end of your rope, tie a knot and hang on.

Franklin D. Roosevelt

Once our minds are 'tattooed' with negative thinking, our chances for long-term success diminish

John Maxwell

Success is relative. It is what we can make of the mess we have made of things.

T. S. Eliot

Success is to be measured not so much by the position that one has reached in life as by the obstacles which one has overcome while trying to succeed.

Booker T. Washington

Success is how high you bounce when you hit bottom.

George S. Patton

It is only as we develop others that we permanently succeed.

Harvey S. Firestone

The men whom I have seen succeed best in life always have been cheerful and hopeful men; who went about their business with a smile on their faces; and took the changes and chances of this mortal life like men; facing rough and smooth alike as it came.

Charles Kingsley

The starting point of all achievement is desire. Weak desire brings weak results.

Napoleon Hill

No bees, no honey; no work, no money.

Proverb

If A equals success, then the formula is: $A = X + Y + Z$, X is work. Y is play. Z is keep your mouth shut.

Albert Einstein

We do not quit playing because we grow old, we grow old because we quit playing.

Oliver Wendell Holmes

ABOUT THE AUTHORS

Stacey Alcorn

Stacey Alcorn has a background in both mortgages and real estate. She started in the mortgage business in 1993 while attending Bentley College. Upon graduating with a Bachelors of Science degree in Accounting, she began originating mortgages with great success. From 1999-2005 she was Senior Vice President of the 13th largest bank holding firm in the United States. In 2000 she purchased her first real estate office and now, with her business partner Andrew Armata, owns multiple offices in Massachusetts and New Hampshire. In 2007 Stacey was nominated as Broker/Owner of the Year by the regional franchise, RE/MAX of New England, and in March of 2008 she was awarded by RE/MAX International for owning the top recruiting RE/MAX real estate office in the United States. In 2005 she and her business partner acquired Unlimited Mortgage. Since then, she has also acquired several other businesses including a title company, a debt servicing organization, and a marketing/promotional firm. In 2007 Stacey was sworn into the Massachusetts Bar Association and now practices pro bono legal services in her spare time.

Andrew F. Armata

Andrew Armata has successfully grown his real estate firm to be the ninth largest in Massachusetts according to the Boston Business Journal. He holds a Bachelors Degree from Northeastern University and he comes from a business management background. While attending Northeastern Andrew opened and ran a well respected commercial property management company. He became partner and CEO of RE/MAX Prestige in 2004 and was successful in doubling the company profits and agent count in less than one year. In 2007 Andrew was nominated as Broker/Owner of the Year by his regional franchise, RE/MAX of New England, and in March of 2008 he was awarded by RE/MAX International for becoming the top recruiting RE/MAX real estate office in the United States. Andrew is widely respected as a real estate expert and has regularly appeared in print and other media outlets. In addition to owning multiple real estate offices in Massachusetts and New Hampshire, Andrew is also a partner in a mortgage brokerage firm, a title closing company, a debt service organization, and a marketing/promotional firm.

Jeff Wright

Jeff Wright graduated from The United States Military Academy at West Point in 1979 and served as an officer in US Army until 1984 attaining the rank of Captain. During that time Jeff received his MBA from Oklahoma City University. While serving on active duty, Jeff began his real estate career in 1980 with an ERA franchise in Lawton, OK. In 1987, Jeff had relocated to his hometown of Trumbull, CT and opened his own real estate firm The Wright Company, Realtors. In 1997 Jeff merged his firm with an existing RE/MAX franchise, RE/MAX United of Trumbull and Shelton, CT and at the same time acquired RE/MAX Preferred of Monroe, CT forming RE/MAX Right Choice. Jeff became the sole owner of RE/MAX Right Choice in December 2001 with 38 agents. In September 2003 RE/MAX Realty Associates of Milford, CT and their 22 agents merged into RE/MAX Right Choice and in February 2006 he bought RE/MAX Action of Stratford, CT with 18 agents. Today RE/MAX Right Choice has 105 agents and does approximately 500 million in annual sales. In 2003 Jeff was named RE/MAX New England Multi-Office Broker/Owner of the year. In 2007 RE/MAX Right Choice had the distinct honor of being selected as one of 6 firms that was named a Great Office by RE/MAX International. Jeff is a member of the RE/MAX Hall of Fame, Chairman's Club and a recipient of the RE/MAX

Lifetime Achievement Award, and his team was in the top 100 teams of RE/MAX International in 2002, 2003 and 2004. In 2007 the team was in the top 100 United States teams.

The Real Estate Playbook Series

For Agents
Playbook of Healthy Time Management - 2009
Playbook of Superstar Lead Generation – Coming January of 2009

For Broker/Owners
Playbook of Talent Acquisition – 2009
Playbook of Retention Success – 2009
Playbook of Mergers & Acquisitions – 2009

For information on speaking, coaching, seminars, and workshops, contact Andrew and Stacey at:

RE/MAX Prestige
211 Chelmsford Street
Chelmsford, MA 01824
Tel.:978-251-8221
Fax: 978-935-9695
Email: AArmata@remax.net
SAlcorn@remax.net

www.RemaxPrestige.com
www.PlayBookSeries.com

Made in the USA
Columbia, SC
24 February 2021